Alight

ALSO BY FADY JOUDAH

<small>POETRY</small>

Textu
The Earth in the Attic

<small>TRANSLATIONS</small>

Like a Straw Bird It Follows Me (poems by Ghassan Zaqtan)
If I Were Another (poems by Mahmoud Darwish)
The Butterfly's Burden (poems by Mahmoud Darwish)

FADY JOUDAH *Alight*

COPPER CANYON PRESS

PORT TOWNSEND, WASHINGTON

Copper Canyon Press is in residence at Fort Worden State Park in Port Townsend,
Washington, under the auspices of Centrum. Centrum is a gathering place for artists
and creative thinkers from around the world, students of all ages and backgrounds, and
audiences seeking extraordinary cultural enrichment.

LIBRARY OF CONGRESS CATALOGING-IN-PUBLICATION DATA

Joudah, Fady, 1971–
  [Poems. Selections]
  Alight / Fady Joudah.
    pages ; cm.
  ISBN 978-1-55659-422-9 (pbk. : alk. paper)
  I. Title.

  PS3610.O679A78 2013
  811'.6—dc23

                    2013003487

98765432 FIRST PRINTING

Copper Canyon Press

Post Office Box 271

Port Townsend, Washington 98368

www.coppercanyonpress.org

ACKNOWLEDGMENTS

The American Poetry Review: "A Line for Water"

Anti-: "Memory Full," "Abundance"

Banipal (UK): "Mimesis," "Also," "I Was There"

Bat City Review: "Hands"

Beloit Poetry Journal: "Tenor"

Callaloo: "Garden"

Field: "After"

Grist: "For," "Decadence"

Harvard Review: "The Security Level Is Yellow"

Indiana Review: "Blue Fly"

The Kenyon Review: "Still Life," "Smoke," "Twice a River"

The Massachusetts Review: "I Was There"

Narrative: "Crow on Saccharine"

New American Writing: "Holy Numbers"

PEN America: "Checkpoint," "A Kindness"

Perihelion: "Birth," "Sleep"

Ploughshares: "Schoolgirl"

Poetry Review (UK): "Museum"

Poetry Society of America: "The Very Hungry Caterpillar"

Poets for Living Waters: "Who Has No Land Has No Sea"

The Rumpus: "Záhrada"

Tex!: "Listening," "Mimesis"

Third Coast: "Border," "Water Proof"

TriQuarterly Online: "In the Picture," "Into Life"

The Wolf (UK): "Holy Numbers"

I would also like to thank the editors of the following anthologies and periodicals, in which some of the poems have been reprinted: *Against Agamemnon; Al-Mutanabbi Street Starts Here; The Best American Poetry 2011; Findings on Elasticity; Human Architecture; Improbable Worlds; Poetry Daily; Seeking Palestine.*

For Mona, the major inspiration for this book,
and for Hana and Ziyad

CONTENTS

One scream the motive for wandering movement

John Taggart

Alight

Tenor

To break with the past
Or break it with the past
The enormous car-packed
Parking lot flashes like a frozen body
Of water a paparazzi sea
After takeoff

And because the pigeons laid eggs and could fly
Because the kittens could survive
Under the rubble wrapped
In shirts of the dead

And the half-empty school benches
Where each boy sits next
To his absence and holds him
In the space between two palms
Pressed to a face/
This world this hospice

After

Over treasure and land some texts will say it had
Little to do with slavery or the newly
Discovered yellow planet

Few men watched the glaciers recede
From shuttles they had built
During the hemorrhage years
When they'd gathered all the genes down from the ledges

I'll be a fig or a sycamore tree
Or without hands

By then doctors and poets
Would have found a cure for prayer

*

Or have you shoved the door shut
In the face of the dark?

Have you body and light the trap
Of retribution doing unto you

What it does to others? You protest
In the streets and papers and I leave

For a faraway land
Where with pill and scalpel

And a distant reckoning
If he should lick his lips

Or clench his fist I shall find his second left toe
Infected puffy

From a bump
I'll lance it and squeeze

Out the pus and offer
Him an antibiotic

I can't refuse therefore I am

*

The first time I saw you it was hot I was fed up
The second time your wife gave birth to a macerated boy

I had nothing to tell you
About letting go of the dying
In the morning you were gone

Had carried your father back to your house
His cracked skull
I didn't know that was your wife
When I raised my voice

To those who were praying
From behind the wall to keep it down

I was trying to listen to your baby's heartbeat
With a gadget a century old

*

Anemic
From so much loss giving birth

If you give blood in the desert you won't
Get it back not your iron pills or magic hat
I put your thin
Hemoglobin up to the light and called out

To the donors Donors
If you want to know your blood type
And it's a match
You must donate

Few came some indifferent to my condition
Not having heard of it
And willing anyhow

*

And the world is south
The night a bandit with gasoline

And I'm your dancing lizard mirth
I put my one arm up
And bring my one foot down on a hot zinc top
The nearest hospital was the dawn

She didn't know her daughter on her back was
The entry wound and she the exit

She ran a brothel so
The officer said

Where the rebels came and went
And ran into the government boys

Her girl's femur the size of the bullet

*

He was from the other side rumors
Had a bullet through his left arm
Or had it bitten off by a camel

A camel elephant of the desert never forgets what you are
If you aren't kind to it

When I met him his bladder was the size
Of a watermelon his prostate a cantaloupe
You cannot catheterize
A man forever

Every hour on the hour his left arm stump
Hanging his good arm holding
His penis his buttocks in deep squeeze
A charge from the rear without spillage

This poor murderous thief desperately single-
Handedly began slapping his own ass
As if he were dashing a stallion in a raid
On some unarmed village

*

The mind in the field
The brine in the field

Whether *I*
Is a diphthong codependent on

What isn't there to stay in the field
The good you act is equal

To the good you doubt
Most have lost many

You are either prosperous
Or veteran in the field

*

A mother offers not necessarily
Sells her one-eyed son

For an education if you'll bring him back
And stone dust for one
With congenital illness

And little boy with malaria
Same old gas

Money mixed with blood
Transfusion the doctor's perfect record broken

Nobility of taking
A life you

Who must walk to and from your house
The jeep's upkeep
The donkey-cart ambulance

*

One boot left behind

The one-boot photo I wanted
On a book military black the quad a clinic's

Special Forces spun
By his dangling heels from

The pickup truck rushed
To a central town altered combative

With two scalp lacerations and blood
In his auditory canal

I was a lover of loss I tossed
The boot in the capital of suffering

Listening

His rage is from not killing anyone at close range, not seeing the brain splatter. He says he was trained to murder but all he did was ride the Humvee probability, and off the record he flipped grenades at villages by the side of the road and laughed, bullet-littered the land and the vehicles passing by when his was passing by. Sometimes he dragged passengers out and mashed them "without touching the face." Sometimes when he walks into a gas station, now that he's back, they greet him: "How are you, brother?" And he replies under his breath, "I am not your fucking brother you gas station people are only targets to me." His is a professional failure. I empathize. He works out but it's in math class that his thoughts wander. He imagines a trespasser, how he'd mutilate him and hide the "microscopic blood." He's tearful, hyperventilates, his mother's shoulder is Siamese with his. "Think of life" I say, he says, "Life is short." I say, "Short or long, think of life," then I go back to my desk where there's a message for me to call my father. I call and he says your sister had penciled something down in Arabic a while back, splotched now. I say, "I don't want to return to anyone. I don't want to return to any country after this long absence. I want only to return to my language in the distances of cooing."

Mimesis

My daughter
            wouldn't hurt a spider
That had nested
Between her bicycle handles
For two weeks
She waited
Until it left of its own accord

If you tear down the web I said
It will simply know
This isn't a place to call home
And you'd get to go biking

She said that's how others
Become refugees isn't it?

Schoolgirl

The love rose in my heart has wilted
The love bug

The news on the transistor
A nice man with a ponytail says

It's understandable
If you wanted to leave here for there

They were burying the evidence
Structurally

Boys in prison cells
And outside the kids play stretcher

One of them was dying
Between my hands you think

Commands injections things
To make the time pass

As hope or action
She used to chase lovebugs after school

To make them alight on her
She wanted not to have

Walked with naked men chained to a tank

In the houses she entered
A lemon an olive an apricot

Hands

If not the swallows in the morning then the smell of guano at night permeating her room, emanating from the bridge where protesters ignite vigils the homeless don't mind.

She no more believes the devil each time it appears that it wants her, no more a girl in line for rationed bread admonished by women who say the soldiers have commenced the rapes.

The soldiers knocked and her father said I'll shoot you if they as much as touch you. She said If you want to shoot someone shoot yourself.

Also

Those who would later be scraped off their seats or
If scorched in retreat scooped up by bulldozers
Then buried in the desert can be seen

In carefully orchestrated pocketknife
Slashes over his distal left forearm

On which his right hand learned
The exact press so that no tendon
Artery or sheath is sliced but enough
For conversation and suture of two

And his boys ten and fifteen
They want to be closer to him more
Than he can let them

Border

To seduce memory
Into song
To twist it
In a twister county

And in turn
Internally displace it
Base it
In the basement

The trees overtake
The streets shave off
Twigs and leaves

And covered in green
The city appears
As forest
Deserted for many years

For years
I reach the story
No one around
A desk in the cellar

The orange peel
Its thick pulp
A day's meal

Checkpoint

He diagrams alleys and where houses stood
Two kilometers from the sea

He is two
One who walks his pencil

Where his feet once walked and one
In the archives of state

There'll be
No repatriation

Only the ghost of place or a shrine
Of a holy man who may or may not

Have passed through the place
As wheat or orange groves

Or one with his donkey and one
Who holds his cigarette in the web

Of the 3rd and 4th fingers
(And for a while this became the fashion

Of the young smokers in the camp)
To pass
The old man must first kiss his donkey's rump

A show of love to what you love
And he made him sing

Still Life

You write your name on unstained glass
So you're either broken or seen through

When it came time for the affidavit
The panel asked how much art
Over the blood of strangers the word

Mentioned the weather and the sleepers
Under the weather all this
Was preceded by tension enzymatic
To the hills behind us and the forests ahead

Where children don't sleep
In resting tremor and shelling
The earth is a pomegranate

A helmet ochre or copper sinks
In buoyant salt water
Divers seek its womb despite its dura mater
And it hangs on trees like pregnant mistletoes

I'll stand next to one
And have my German lover

Remember me on a Mediterranean island
Though she would eventually wed
An Israeli once she'd realized
What she wanted from life

A mother of two
On the nose of Mount Carmel
Where my wife's father was born driven out

My father's hands depearl
The fruit in a few minutes add a drop
Of rose water some shredded coconut
For us to gather around him

He will lead his grandchildren out transfer
Bundles of pine branches in the yard to where
His tomatoes and cucumbers grow in summer

Let them let them
Gather the dried pine needles forever he says
They will refuse to believe the fire dies

And they will listen to his first fire
On a cold night in a forest of eucalyptus trees
The British had planted as natural reserve
Outside Gaza

A Kindness

Taxi driver drives through Main his plates are legit
A father and son in the shadow of snipers

To pray surrounded by guards
To pray to the guards or
To the invisible god in the guards or the one surrounding the guards

Among the rubble I send them
Caterpillars that eat their mothers and taxed pronouns

Does your house have a gardener
How long around the wall?
Our age is a checkpoint

We grieve like palm trees by the river
Dance like palm trees by the river
We reach the pigeon coop check on the pigeons the pigeons fly

Son finds a stray puppy calls to it in his enemy's tongue
Taxi exits Broadway
Son poses like a kid in the shadow of snipers

Memory Full

If it were autumn the leaves would in their butterfly dance belly-up as they hit the grass and become reservoir for rain or dew or black boots that ask you about your father: your sweat rolls like grape leaves or rosary beads neglected in some trinket box your great-grandmother bought in Mecca a century ago, having counted the pillars in the mosque as evidence she'd been there. Some idle talk on the bus. And in comes the cockroach in his summer trunks fibrillating his limbs to an atavistic rhythm while your neighbor's leg hairs are weeping willows in the compound pool. In the blue bus that swallowed the heat the heat was a leavened carcass. But your father knew the rules: you're still a minor, and water still had dreams for you in wooden cartons on Thursday afternoons, figs the likes of which you haven't tasted since.

Siblings

My sister tones up her soul when she laughs
Try it and you might break a rib or two

Once I made her laugh a stream of gold
That shot down between her feet
And with roast-beef knife in hand
My brother took off running after me

Maybe he just loved to hear my girly scream

Maybe it's true I was the one
Who pushed him off the ground-floor balcony

When we were toddlers
And shattered his elbow
The one the surgeon broke and rebroke
Left deformed and mentionable

To beat him
To the bathroom door wasn't enough
You had to shut it behind you
Turn and hold force against force

Without doubting how much of it
There really was on the other side

Smoke

With a cigarette in her left hand she says love built the gazebo

Thirty years after the smoke between the two clans had cleared
His from a village meaning little planet
In the coastal plains hers from the city of golden locks

They were off to a faraway country of immigrants
No blood was shed no wedding only marriage

Then her husband sought identity in manuscripts
At the oldest campus on another continent

There were riots the philosophers had joined the students
Fumes arched and landed into the cuff of his pants
It had been the first time he'd seen tear-gas

Bombs even though he was among those who
Decades prior had burned down an ancient capital

He flicked his leg and sent the bomb flying into the crowd

He's next to her now
Her secondhand smoke

Even if he was once caught in a street battle during a civil war
He rushed inside the first door

That would open a madam greeted him and offered
One of her girls for a fee and in a second he

Was back out on the street
Said he had scripts to write and scrolls to find

In the Picture

In the picture that wasn't taken
I lost my arthritis and started running

But was still
Overrun by the sea

As if I had been faking it all along
My bad knees stiff pelvis as if

I had been cured of wheelchair or cane
Evangelized prosthetized
And the world broke into laughter

I leapt over a high wall to flee
The patrol then ran for miles

On a twisted ankle without pain

I would have walked in water
Were it not for a donkey

Blowing up on the shore a land mine
On the edge of sand and foam

I would have held you in my arms
Would've smelled of algae for days

I Was There

I was there only once
Under the rock I touched the rock

And did not fly did not believe
The rock could fly or hover
With the air propped up by a wall

The key was cypress wood or willow wood
I don't remember

Time buried in hills
"Perhaps buried till
Some happier age" time

What is holy or cleansing
A rusty water fountain
Bled me

And I did not contract tetanus
Gold didn't concern me or turning olives into gold

As if I were an alchemist outside chrome
Doors of houses we wear
In dementia like a palindrome

Museum

Photographs with bullet holes face up
Or down all nude
And if alive then with priapism
Or many vaginal views
An anagram between cover-up and exposition

If the catastrophe goes on a man
Comes into focus
In his enemy's eyes when they meet

As expecting fathers a mother speaks
Exactly of the moment
A newborn rips her groin or lacerates
Her nipples later on

And the vagrant shivers deep
Into the viscera and up into the arteries of sleep
Your syncopated bit

That throws her down
As in a baptism her legs raised
And propped up by your legs like a table
Thighs through the camel's needle
Or when the highway wind
Meets up with another wind heaving a pigeon

The thud a prelude
That leaves behind no feathers
Or blood on the hood
Only a crippled bird in grocery store parking lot
Vying for morsels

Or pheasants
On dirt roads after curfew
Intoxicated by the sight headlights reveal

Holy Numbers

I

A bird flu over the city by night
Boom's an owl and not just any owl

You carry the plight over the gulf
Of convalescence to an ecotourism
After the massacre then masquerade
As keeper of zoo and museum
And woe the senses of children and neighbors
And guilty conquerors who stitch

The railroad-track textile skin by day
And hitch with a long sleeve in summer
Or a wide watchband your ruins on job
Interview as all good things are country
The big city embraces in boom

Your enemy becomes your lover

2

Pastoral or industrial I wear grass
After mowing the lawn and long for
The buried well in the orange grove
Watermelon and a grapevine trellis

Come the season a helicopter will
Release the little prince's enuresis
A blue collar of the dove or the leaf of
The iceberg two coves down from

Nom de guerre/ you tube we cut and paste
To digital space isotopes at the gates
Of our wedding to stranger women

And dogs of faraway slums/ the disorder
Mirror was deductible agreed upon
Documentary lesser than fiction

3

In the parking lot of the gated comm-
Unity its repair and maintenance team
I light my cigarette after I get up get dressed
Face the wall and raise my arms up like this
Then head to the bank

Though not before the hallway fumes of carpet-
Cleaning meet and choke me and I become
A unionist on a confederate task

And say to the cleaning lady Why
Don't you ask for a mask but she nods it's okay!

In front of the bank a homeless woman
Wears different eyes for smoke in December
Half a cigarette in a cement crack
One stranger's mouth to another's

4

The sewing machine pedals like a machine
Gun in a city in war the shooting from
A nearby neighborhood or so you imagine
In a city in war or at it you have never
Lived lived as in called it yours when
One battalion replaced another
It made a similar sound fifteen
Minutes straight to let you know
What it was like/ we squatted in the room
With the four ventilation slits high up
Near the ceiling and kept our calm chat that
After all it was a brick wall and where we
Stayed we rented from a local merchant
Who could afford to fire mud into brick

5

Still I make certain to round up redemption
Daily healing maybe I regurgitate
Too much the events of the day my own
Split multitudes in nanomirrors

Shut out the false world I hear but I wasn't
Born there and here I want to shake the hands
Of those I've wronged and who've wronged me first
If I chicken well I might egg better

All beauty is co-optation of affliction
Though never say all or never
Your oath's your oath and if in this world
You should bear two daughters you'd enter heaven

And trust the nonstop flight
For forty vernal days and forty autumnal nights

6

Two Earths the one uninhabited by
Humans diagnoses the other with
Severe eczema prescribes a topical steroid
Two Earths one super-bad one super-
Model on a jet plane examine a third's
Chalked and charred dermatomes
Where shingles linger two Earths on a stage

The one playing watermelon says to
The one playing garlic No man could ever
Come near you the garlic says But I don't
Go home with whoever pats me on the ass
Two Earths against revenge count their dead
The way the Pink Panther split his loot
One for you one for me two for you one two for me

7

Then come visions and numinous visitations
I take the steps and am off
A goose sojourn a quack in the wilderness

I've been known to streak the shore and moon
The waterfall anecdotal less reliable
Than cohort a faulty vortex
In gregarious flock a pack
Of cigarettes a month is a wineglass a day

I play a prophet Cabernet
In hand someone says the poetry postcard had
The lateness of olive trees written on the back of it
I thought none of it

I washed the carrots then fed the horse
And couldn't raise my eyes above my brows

Blue Fly

You dream of a pony. You have a fear of flies. Houseflies, horseflies, greenflies, you name it. There was a famous warrior poet once, his name was Blue Fly. Perhaps because that's the most elusive kind of jinn, blue jinn: *"And I remembered you as spears quenched their thirst / in me and swords gleamed as white as your smile."* Except you are staring at a colossal fly poised on the bench, while the trainer places a blue bicycle helmet on your head for the pony ride, and you ask, How is this going to protect me from the fly! The trainer calmly replies, Last week I rode an Arabian horse for 500 miles and was all right. But you can't believe it, traveling all that distance while swatting at flies.

The Very Hungry Caterpillar

After gluttony the insatiable rain

Drowns the earth and all the ruins
Remain cannot be finished off

You climb up to the highest post
A lemon tree

You become visible suspected at first
Of being bird excrement
Its odd landing

Visible through the kitchen window
Of all who can dislocate you from a leaf

To the concrete with a twig
And unsure what you believe

When jabbed when your red-horned tongue flashes
Out of your grotesque head

I poke you writhe
A green juice out of you the color

Of the earth you ravaged
Mint and thyme

The next day the sun
The rest of your clan
A festival on branches

Your cranium a Worf's
Your future a swallowtail

Crow on Saccharine

We boarded a ferry to a promised shore

Reached the shore and twirled our wrists

Spanish dancers or some folk from the East
Eager for foaming water rushing toward our feet

Two pigeons in a pine tree

Two city pigeons straightening out each other's feathers
After the afternoon showers

Wasn't that a friend's eureka while dancing at our wedding

Unable to move his hips he shouted
It's all in the hands all in the hands?

A maid made my bed each day I was a humanitarian
And did not wake up next to you

Here we leave our bed undone

For

Shall we have another child then?
Our daughter could use a sibling

Our parents would be grand
It's neither truth nor lie the immortality love brings

A bunched-up mirror of cells
That form and reform
For a reason or when reason ceases
To preside over a good thing

For an age when
We are likely to have little to occupy

Being in time with being good to a child

Not for now but for
A hundred years from now

What one love one could not love well enough
To want the same for another

Abundance

And what shall we name him/ an eggplant in the ubiquitous joints/ an addendum to Andalusia/ a troubled succession of vowels/ to plague the white horse you rode on like a mouse/ twice flung we followed on foot/ the sidewalk was hood after hood/ or teeth/ an accent barred from being/ elected president/ we mulled it over the wild blue rasp/ stuck to the end of a straw/ whose back we've got/ a house to displace in an up-and-coming district/ and in the organic market/ spelled/ in line for power that had gone out/ for eggs ice and dairy we could afford/ what the cashier couldn't/ an aubergine/ a nicotine-filled berry

Birth

I

Three sparrows in the schoolyard while waiting for my daughter to finish up her play with friends whose purity she will come to question in a few weeks and in that way I am reminded of the president when he speaks of enemies to the other side of the mirror but only in that way the three sparrows ruffled up the dirt as their wings and heads spun motorbike doughnuts after one of them had come back with a massive potato chip for the other two to fight over perhaps he was the provider or wasn't hungry but simply couldn't let a good bit of food go to waste

Then a crow came and the winner sparrow went zooming into the orange orchard knowing fully well it would be impossible to alight and reappeared with a chip the size of his beak and a flurry of birds descended on the scene (I even saw a Fletcher) but kept my eyes on that little sparrow and am happy to report he kept what his mouth held though it occurs to me he was also mean and the one who seemed a provider might have been yoked in that way my wife during delivery was rung up like a bar code whenever the nurse knocked or the doctor was called

2

In the room there were women
Counting up to ten dressed in blue
The doctor was also
Pregnant in her final week

The neonate came out broke
The sound barrier and was whisked
Away from the mother the father
Had cut the cord having held

Scissors before he couldn't turn down
The doctor's offer as if he would
Have denied someone an entry
Or exit visa

Then the women were gone
And neighbors and friends had to go
To work and the mother was alone
With breast or formula milk

One nurse suggested the latter
Was the better soporific

3

An infant smile
A gas tickle
The price of milk

It goes up in war

My son is here to teach me
My temperament is genetic

His smile is blind
It dreams a spandrel
Turns opiate in the eyes

He grunts impatient wants
Gas out as soon as

It forms in peace
He coos

It's what doves do
Though excitable
Observant of moving lips

Attempts utterance
Throws up happy spit
And hunger's renewed

Záhrada

From the Moorish synagogue in Prague
Next to Kafka's statue
The father wife and daughter headed to the cemetery

Death that has never been to the orthodontist
Death hiding death burying death Frankfurt Judengasse
Gates an echo nearby

They walked the streets and cubic cobblestones
The size of olive soap bars
From Nablus fascinated the child's down-drawn head
She was learning to daydream without stumbling

Look up the father said but she kept
Her gaze on the stones they the teeth she the fairy

She will carry one back with her on the plane
Another's national treasure
The family will be greeted then asked to step aside
In a language they speak when home alone

On the bathroom mantel the stone will come to rest
Her sink is next to her mother's sink
But the father remembers it differently

The word for *garden* was it
Borrowed from another's tongue whose soldiers
And lovers were never in the galas this far north?

Or maybe from a time before the great diversions
Like *cornea* or *cave* or *earth*?

Sometimes the girl is disinterested in the cognate world
And she forgets all about the stones she's gathered
From different summers

Waterproof

How did the time pass
When all we had was
The flow of sense and body
Embrace without pose
For a fossiliferous world
Where the camera fell
In the water of a waterfall
We wanted badly framed
And now its lack is what submits
To memory

Or were those days always there in the war
Its smithereens of your family's
Photo album as you gather
Around now and over a picture that remains
Of the selves that are here
And the selves that are gone

Sleep

For years I have known her an old woman
A nurse's aide she always says good morning
And not until my son was born did she share this with me

In her wallet two photos one of a ten-pound baby
Her firstborn who shot himself accidentally
Playing with a gun when he was twelve

In Cyprus the Trojan side at a café
An old woman approached me a teenager then
And said I looked like her dead son

I have a familiar face
And despite what my mother or sister say
These dreams aren't for construal

I leap from my sleep to visceral
Sounds my newborn makes in his sleep
I wrap his torso in the frond of my palm and watch
My father's breathlessness then his gasp

A woman wrote over and over in precise
Short poems the five stages of grief

It began a few mornings after she walked in
On her son dead in his sleep

I am older now I bear the news
Of a son's death to his mother
He was the weaker of the twins I say
It wasn't anything you did or didn't do

What was it then! she asks
And I can only answer her in my sleep

Poem

Like a rock climber my son pivots

His feet against my back

Or belly in the middle of the night

He has returned to occupy

Our bed my wife's and mine

Distance us from our nightly chores

We forget who we are

Become insomniac

His recurrence a soldier's

Impending distress if addressed or not addressed

It competes with that of the occupied

My son wants to feel warm

Smell the smell of love

Digs deeper to remind me

His toenails are a week too long

Decadence

August, air-conditioned swamp city, a mosquito made itself manifest after we'd shut the doors, got on our way, the baby fastened in his rear-facing seat. It wasn't long before we parked at the shoulder of the road and let the ass-huggers behind us pass. We were free to swipe at the lone mosquito, hemi-ballistic, just as our son would at things and nonthings if such a thing exists. Or perhaps we mimicked chorea: pronounced like the state so frequently mentioned, though it comes with options. As in, I once saved a girl from chorea, or I once got a boy out of chorea (which takes no more than a few shots). But there would be no moving on unless the mosquito was dead. The cabin completely sealed. We wanted a rectangular mortality, an impartial falling at line's end.

Garden

"Death makes angels of us all"
I'd written on the blackboard in the cadaver room

The next morning someone wrote Are you sure?
If not angels then flowers I said then flew

To the town of holy taverns
Where beggars prostrate for hours

Until one sits straight up head engorged like a lily
On fast-forward in a nature show

At the bed-and-breakfast
The owner served us crab quiche
The nearby pueblo was closed that day

A mother kept shouting Go back Go back
So we rode a tour bus to the levee

"Mean ol' levee taught me to weep and moan"
And the old man with crummy pockets snapped

Son this lottery ticket's expired!
No matter here's some money for it

But if it wins dear sir the hobo said
Forget me not forget me not

"Who Has No Land Has No Sea"

If the catastrophe goes on it has gone on dragonflies
Will mime mummify in despair until one grows
An aardvark's tongue licks its wings and legs free
To procreate new lines of flight and the egret
Now a brown duck will find a ship or a rock on which to dock
Beguiled and perplexed like someone saved from drowning
Though not from Poseidon's beasts no use trying
To hose its feathers down no down or downtime
For this one bird when sight is set on the future
Of a thousand other birds who quickly learn from the drift
Carcasses and dolphin logs and from those who have survived
Who will perish in their intoxicated plumes like sleeping
Under car hoods in a mechanic's garage for 5,000 miles
On end oil change and gulf jumbo shrimp gulping
If all is one one is not all the earth always wins for losing

Twice a River

After studying our faces for months
My son knows to beam
Is the thing to do

He'll spend years deciphering love
The injustice or the illusion
Having been brought into this world
Volition is an afterthought

What will I tell him
About land and language and burial
Places my father doesn't speak of
Perhaps my mother knows

In the movie the dispossessed cannot return
Even when they're dead
The journalist felt

Rebuke for not having thought
It mattered or for having thought it mattered too much

Will I tell my son all nations arise after mass
Murder that I don't know

Any national anthem by heart can't sing
"Take Me Out to the Ball Game"?

I should turn to flowers and clouds instead
Though this has already been said well
It is night

When he gazes
Into his mother's eyes at bath time
Qyss & Laila she announces after a long day's work

He giggles with his shoulders not knowing
He's installing a web

In his amygdala or whichever
Places science thinks love dwells

Even love is a place? O son
Love no country and hate none
And remember crimes sometimes

Immortalize their victims
Other times the victimizer

Remember how you used to gaze at the trampoline
Leaves on their branches?

Don't believe the sound of the sea
In a seashell believe the sea
The endless trope and don't say

Much about another's language
Learn to love it

While observing silence
For the dead and the living in it

The Bedouin Poem

The moon, a pure Islamic shape, looked down.
T. Roethke

A fish in the tank, you say, is better than ten at sea, but it simply ate all the other fishes in the tank, grew huge and ugly, and when looked up on the net, it turned out edible, a delicacy, in fact, in some true marine community.

The Bedouin man put on a pair of flowery kitchen-sink gloves, his wife and her children cheered his fearful hands (he's a stepdad).

The fish plopped out to hardwood floor sound-effect on a Texas farm, or maybe it was carpet: grilled and a memory, all who were in the room wolfed it, except the daughter who was startled out of sleep unto the scene, and the grandmother who "like a Mohammedan still wears her thick lavender mourning and touring veil."

Later, the wife and children wanted a dog. To convince the Bedouin they told him the puppy of litter and giveaways they had found was instead one abandoned in a cemetery on burial day, where an old bereft woman was kneeling "in her Sunday black dress and touching the ground with her forehead like a Mohammedan." Now, in love, the Bedouin naps on the floor with the puppy by his armpit.

In his mother's house there was room for anyone at the last supper. Such is time, a hound or a pit bull, what names may bring. The dog never barks at a soul in town whom the dead mother knew, loved or didn't.

A Line for Water

All morning we spoke
        the imagined was probable

                future but also mentioned
                specifics like freedom of hair

                design and the art of kissing a cheek

We drove around the neighborhood toilet
        paper ribboned the live oak

                we stopped by the distressed
                magnolia as a town-

                home was being
                built by its north face

                the earth was thin over the deep root

I left the car fuming
        stepped out to see the tree was blooming

                on all heights all around
                let's go back you said

                before more ice melts and the polar bear
                would fight the grizzly

                in a documentary
                we'd have to make

But radio stations don't keep
    the same frequency across state lines

        the colonel said things other colonels say
        they marched were marched

        through maize fields in July
        sucked but the maize was dry

        and thirst was donkey-piss thirst

A boy didn't know how to swim
    jumped in a well

        when his parched mother told him
        this would be the day she'd die

        and the marched pulled him out

        sucked his clothes then were marched
        a boy

        asked a guard for some water went
        into seizure and never came back

We'd had enough of the interior
    the bathroom photo of children

        frolicking in a fountain
        in a city where mothers vote

        we got our family picture taken our hair cut
        our subdivision's catch-and-release

        pond was given a fountain two
        pairs of ducks and herons

we tried to capture in flight on camera
for schoolwork the dumb fishes swam about

with punctured lips
not having learned from their previous errors

A poet was a soldier once
and is now forgiven

a chicken crossed the road to listen
to some Bach Bach you said and desert

is one of water's names
showers from wells we dig

skin cracks that stomp the ground
till God blows up

an aquifer beneath the feet
soda-orange water the sand had settled in

or another untouchable soil
let loose from the conquered hills

animals killing farms
women and young girls jump

up and down the water pump
handle an oil drill

smiling how beautiful their toned arms

We rode through the fountain
	on leaf-blower mornings

	walked in the heat collapsed
	and needed to be hung

	to drips and were
	wild in the movies

We swapped our strollers for slings
	and were jigsaw-puzzled on the thoroughfare

	and the baby with the bathwater
	we bibbed were bibbed

	ran loads in the washer
	love's no policy

	the think-tank man said over dinner and wine
	and wine is a diuretic

A boy walked back to his village
	alone carrying nothing in the night
	wolves howled and guns cocked

	a mother toiled the land illiterate
	our eardrums flapped as tarp

	that feeling a mirage a boy
	on a bicycle through checkered

	tree-shadow clearing
	the fog with a machete

A boy out of his upper-end
      house with a wooden sword

      headed for the bamboo
      that landscapes his house

      we were strolling by then
      you were taken

      by trees
      an ancient magnolia

      a giant lemon blossom you called it

The Security Level Is Yellow

Last night is so often where things begin/
Maybe because I saw you on Facebook
Earlier in the day making out with
A friend's status/ or because I had been
Thinking about calligraphy Jackson
Pollock was my pretext/ really he was
A classicist after all following
The fractal of the mind to the rhythms
Of eternal recurrence that bury
And elevate/ open and reopen
The way Jerusalem came to sit on
Jagged mounds/ did you know *nostalgia* was
A recent word in your language?/ you were
Sitting on one of those metal chairs one
Finds in cafeterias or town halls/
Straddling it like a horseman or a lap
Dancer/ shaking your head at a visa-
Less pace in sheer disappointment/
I had been found out/ I'd left a message
On your answering machine intended
For another's/ I said I was sorry
But you kept shaking your head as you drove
Away screechless in your middle-middle-
Class car/ I tried to tell you about that
Time in the Rockies we were three and the wind
Betrayed me down the hill as if it were
A carrier pigeon or a listening
Device/ our third heard everything I
Had said about him but was okay
With it as cool as FYI/ on his
Wedding night/ I stood and toasted the story
As proof of his capacity to love

Into Life

Mouths that breathe like fishes out of water
Faster then slower pursed lips then gaping mouths billowing chests and all

The fixed stare that gives its sense up and over to other sense and reflex

I can't bear it
Am frightened
Of the dorsal fins fanning out to puncture the hand that wants the hook

Out of the mouth to throw the fish back in

I don't blame the fish its indiscriminate violence it cannot know
It was my daughter's hand that threaded the bait and cast the line

She too wants them back in the water
But can't let go of the desire
To catch what she can't see but knows is teeming

An idea of absence a little blue
Heron partakes in and dives after
Each fish I unhook and toss into life

And not once did the bird come up beak-filled or gulping

I eat fish
Same as I eat rabbit

Without nearing the look on its face
When my mother would grab it
By its long ears the blade approaching

Then skinning it by hand like peeling a banana

The fish's pulled out and is plopped on the deck
Fluttering like a startled bird or an epileptic

I pin it down by the gills with my index
Retrieve the hook with my other hand

Then under and across its belly where the spikes are short
I dart it

That's before I thought of a towel

That stare that white light
Of the day's operating theater burning

The retina like a flash without an image
To behold a clean slate a blank page

A summation of color in the final cortex
(Which fishes don't have)

Then the electric shock the pain of coming
Back into life

ABOUT THE AUTHOR

Fady Joudah's *The Earth in the Attic* was selected for the Yale Series of Younger Poets. His translations have received a Banipal Prize in the UK and a PEN Center USA award. He is a doctor of internal medicine in Houston, Texas.

Poetry is vital to language and living. Since 1972, Copper Canyon Press has published extraordinary poetry from around the world to engage the imaginations and intellects of readers, writers, booksellers, librarians, teachers, students, and donors.

WE ARE GRATEFUL FOR THE MAJOR SUPPORT PROVIDED BY:

THE PAUL G. ALLEN
FAMILY FOUNDATION

THE MAURER FAMILY
FOUNDATION

NATIONAL
ENDOWMENT
FOR THE ARTS

Anonymous

Arcadia Fund

John Branch

Diana and Jay Broze

Beroz Ferrell & The Point, LLC

Mimi Gardner Gates

Gull Industries, Inc.
on behalf of William and Ruth True

Mark Hamilton and Suzie Rapp

Carolyn and Robert Hedin

Steven Myron Holl

Rhoady and Jeanne Marie Lee

Maureen Lee and Mark Busto

New Mexico Community Foundation

H. Stewart Parker

Penny and Jerry Peabody

Joseph C. Roberts

Cynthia Lovelace Sears and Frank Buxton

The Seattle Foundation

Charles and Barbara Wright

The dedicated interns and faithful
volunteers of Copper Canyon Press

To learn more about underwriting Copper Canyon Press titles,
please call 360-385-4925 ext. 103

The Chinese character for poetry is made up of two parts:
"word" and "temple." It also serves as pressmark for
Copper Canyon Press.

The poems are set in Fournier.
Book design and composition by Phil Kovacevich.
Printed on archival-quality paper at McNaughton & Gunn, Inc.